Simply Charming
Table of Contents

Pattern	Page Number
Commonly Asked Questions	1
Simply Charming Four Patch	3
Simply Charming Nine Patch	5
Simply Twisted	7
Simply Untwisted	9
Charming Flowers	11
Charming Birds	13
Charming Fat Quarter	15
Charming Queen	17
Charming Squares	19
Charming Fat Triangles	29
Charming Fence	31
The Charming Path	33
Charming Old Maid	35
Charming Lady	37
Charming Baskets	39
Charming Lonestar	41
Appendix A: Half Square Triangles	45
Appendix B: Midge's Perfect Sashing and Borders	46
Appendix C: Piecing a Back	47

©March 2009 Moose on the Porch Quilts. All rights reserved. No portion of this document may be reproduced in any form, except for personal use by the purchaser, or by any means unless permission has been granted by Moose on the Porch Quilts. The content of this book is intended for personal use only and is protected by federal copyright laws.

Moose on the Porch Quilts
Konda Luckau
665 E 400 S, Payson, UT 84651
801-465-9892
www.moosequilts.com

Commonly Asked Questions about Charm Packs:

1) What is a charm pack?
A charm pack is a package of pre cut 5" squares. Generally a charm pack contains between 30 and 40 squares. All of the fabrics are different because the package includes one square of each fabric in a fabric line excluding panels. Some fabric lines have one charm pack that contains the prints of the line and a separate charm pack that contains the woven fabrics which are commonly plaids of a particular line.

2) Where can I buy charm packs?
Most quilt shops carry charm packs. They are also available online. Right now not all fabric manufacturers make charm packs, but more manufacturers will make them as everyone discovers how much fun they are!

3) What can I do with just one charm pack?
Several patterns in this book can be made with just one charm pack! They include *Charming Fat Quarter* and the baby/table topper size of both *Simply Charming Four Patch* and *Simply Charming Nine Patch*. In addition, every quilt in this book can be made using just one charm pack if you make fewer blocks.

4) What if my charm pack doesn't have enough squares in it?
Because the number of fabrics varies in each charm pack, it is impossible to tell the number of charm packs that each pattern will need. If a charm pack is lacking just a few squares, you have a couple options. First you can always buy another charm pack and use the leftovers to make another quilt like the *Charming Fat Quarter* that doesn't take as many charms. Another thing I have done, is purchase a little extra fabric for the borders or binding and cut a couple 5" squares out of the extra yardage.

5) Can I make these patterns without using charm packs?
Absolutely! Here are some places to find 5" squares:
- ~ Cut 5" squares out of your *scraps*. All of these quilt patterns make fabulous scrap quilts.
- ~ Cut 5" squares out of *yardage*. When purchasing yardage for 5" squares, 1/3 yard is a good amount to buy. That will give you two 5" strips with just 2" leftover. These 5" strips can each be cut into 8 squares so 1/3 yard of fabric will give you 16 charm squares.
- ~ Cut 5" squares out of a *fat quarter*. You can cut twelve 5" squares out of one fat quarter with a couple inches leftover. **All the patterns in this book are Fat Quarter Friendly!**

6) What if I want to make the pattern larger?
All of the patterns in this book are very simple to enlarge!

One way to make the patterns larger is to make more blocks. Any pattern that is made up of blocks can be enlarged by making more blocks. When making more blocks for a quilt, be aware of whether the number of blocks in a setting is even or odd. For example, *Simply Twisted* is made up of 24 blocks, 4 across and 6 down. To keep the pattern consistent, I would need to stay with even numbers like 6 across and 8 down or 10 across and 10 down. Some quilts like *Simply Charming Four Patch* and *Simply Charming Nine Patch* don't have a pattern formed by the blocks so it doesn't matter if the number of blocks is even or odd. Another thing to consider when you enlarge a quilt by making more blocks is the size of the border. A quilt that started out with a 4" border will need a larger border if it is made into a queen size quilt. The border should be widened or an additional border should be added to keep the quilt in balance.

Another way to make the quilts larger is to add more borders. This method would work nicely on any of the quilts. One thing to think about when adding borders is that it is more pleasing to the eye to have the borders get larger as they go out. For example, *Charming Flowers* has a 2" border and a 5" border. So the next border would need to be 7" or 8". If that is too much border, then you could also change the borders to be 2", 4", and 6" or something else similar. Keep in mind that borders add width and length quickly.

7) Why should I buy a charm pack?
Here are my top ten reasons to buy charm packs:
1) They are just so fun!
2) To quickly achieve a scrappy look.
3) All the fabrics match.
4) You get a piece of an entire fabric line.
5) The squares are already cut.
6) To say, "Thank you!"
7) To say, "Happy Birthday!"
8) To say, "Merry Christmas."
9) They are quicker gifts than making cookies, less fattening, and last longer.
10) To be adventurous!

The reason I picked up my first charm pack was to be adventurous and stretch myself. I rarely buy plaids or grayed fabrics, but I love the comfortable look of quilts made using these fabrics. I decided to challenge myself to make a plaid quilt. I had a terrible time trying to select these fabrics. I fell in love with all the new brown fabrics that had come out, but I still couldn't get to the plaids. I wasn't brave enough to buy fabric I didn't absolutely love.

That was when I purchased a few of *Moda's Chocolat Wovens Charm Packs*. The result was *Simply Twisted*, and I was hooked! I love that quilt, and I never would have made it if I had to buy the fabrics one at a time. My hand would have passed over at least half of them.

Charm Packs are mini-kits. Someone has put together 30-40 fabrics that look fabulous with each other. Occasionally in a charm pack, there are one or two fabrics that I really don't like. I will usually force myself to sew it into the quilt. Many times I find myself surprised that I like the offending fabric just fine once the quilt is finished because of the dimension and depth it adds to the quilt. Other times, I still don't like it, but there are only one or two in the quilt, so I am not disappointed with the overall result. And often I find that the fabric that I thought was so offensive is exactly the fabric that another person loves. That's part of the fun of quilting!

Good luck! I hope you have as much fun with these patterns as I have had making them.
Thanks, Konda Luckau

Simply Charming Four Patch
Block Size: 9 ½" (9" finished)
Quilt Size: 58" x 69"

This pattern is so super simple and yields such fun results that you will want to make this classic pattern over and over again. The full sized pattern is a short twin which is a size that I love! It is perfect to use on the couch watching television or on a chair reading a book. The baby/table topper size only takes 1 charm pack!

Fabric Requirements:
- 80 charm (5") squares
- 1 yard for 2" sashing
- 1 ¼ yards for 6" border
- 3 ½ yards for backing
- 2/3 yard for binding

Cutting Instructions:
1) From sashing fabric, cut 14-2 ½" strips width of fabric.
   a) Cut 4 of the strips into 15-2 ½" x 9 ½".
   b) Cut 2 of the strips in half.
c) Do not cut the rest of the strips.
2) Cut the border fabric into 6-6 ½" strips width of fabric.

Sewing Instructions:
1) Sew the 80 charm squares into 20 four patch blocks as shown in Figure A. Press.

Figure A

2) After laying out the blocks, sew the vertical sashing pieces onto the right side of the first three four patch blocks in each row as shown in Figure B. Do NOT sew a sashing piece onto the last block.

Figure B

3) Sew each strip together. Press.

4) Refer to Appendix B for instructions on sewing sashing. Sew a horizontal sashing strip to the bottom of the first row as shown in Figure C. Each row is 42½" long so one fabric strip should fit. If it doesn't fit, there is extra from the 4

Figure C

strips you cut in step 2 to add a little on. Sew and press. Continue sewing a sashing strip to the bottom of the second, third, and fourth rows, NOT the last row.

5) Sew the rows together as in Figure D and press.

6) Take the 4 half sashing strips and sew one of the halves onto each of the remaining four strips.

7) Sew on the first border with these sashing strips by first sewing on the side strips and next sewing on the top and bottom strips.

8) Sew the outer border on in the same manner.

9) Refer to Appendix C method 2 to sew backing.

10) Cut 7—2 ½" strips width of fabric for binding.

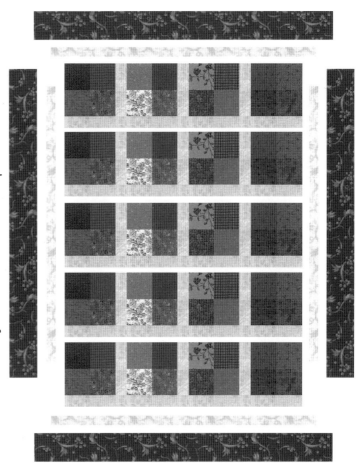

Figure D

Baby Size /Table Topper
42" x 42"
9 ½" block (9" finished)

Fabric Requirements:
- 36 charm (5") squares
- ¾ yard for 2" sashing
- ½ yard for 3 ½" border
- 1 1/3 yards for backing
- ½ yard for binding

Cutting Instructions:
1) From sashing fabric, cut 8-2 ½" strips width of fabric.
    a) Cut 2 of the strips into 6-2 ½" x 9 ½".
    b) Do not cut the rest of the strips.
2) Cut the border fabric into 4-4" strips width of fabric.

Sewing Instructions:
Same sewing instructions as larger size.

Simply Charming Nine Patch
61" x 76 ½"
14" block (13 ½" finished)

This is another classic pattern in a fun, useable size. This baby/table topper size only uses one charm pack! The nine patch unit gives a little more room to play with the colors of the block. You can make them completely scrappy or make a more traditional nine patch block with light and dark colors alternating.

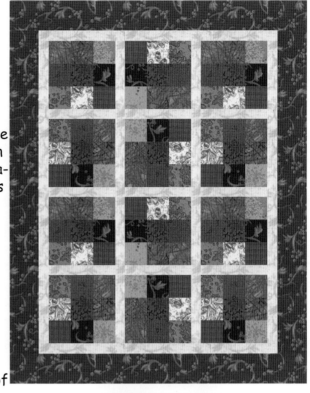

Fabric Requirements:
- 108 charm (5") squares
- 1 ¼ yards for 2" sashing
- 1 1/3 yards for 6" border
- 4 yards for backing
- 2/3 yard for binding

Cutting Instructions:
1) From sashing fabric, cut 14-2 ½" strips width of fabric.
    a) Cut 3 of the strips into 8-2 ½" x 14".
    b) Cut 2 of the strips in half.
    c) Do not cut the rest of the strips.
2) Cut the border fabric into 7-6 ½" strips width of fabric.

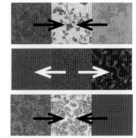

Figure A

Sewing Instructions:
1) Sew the 108 charm squares into 12 nine patch blocks. To do this, first sew three sets of three as shown in Figure A. Then sew these sets together matching the corners. Press seams in the directions of the arrows.

2) After laying out the blocks, sew the 14" vertical sashing pieces onto the right of the first two of the nine patch blocks in each row as shown in Figure B. Do NOT sew a sashing piece onto the last block.

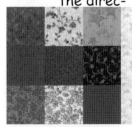

Figure B

3) Sew the three squares together to make a strip as shown in Figure C. Press.

4) Refer to Appendix B for instructions on sewing sashing. Take the 4 half sashing strips and sew onto the end of a whole strips. For the fifth horizontal sashing strip, use the one extra 14" strip from step 2 and sew it onto the end of another strip. Now sew one of these horizontal sashing strips to the bottom of the first row as shown in Figure C. Continue sewing a sashing strip to the bottom of

Figure C

the second and third rows. Do NOT sew a sashing strip on the bottom of the last row. There are two 60" sashing strips left for the top and bottom sashing borders.

5) Sew the rows together and press. The quilt should now measure 45" x 60½".

6) Take the remaining four sashing strips and sew two of them together. Sew another pair together so now there are 2 double sashing strips.

7) Sew on the first border using these double sashing strips for the left side and the right side strips. Next sewing on the top and bottom borders using the sashing strips left over from step 4.

8) Sew the outer border on in the same manner.

9) Refer to Appendix C method 2 to cut and sew the backing fabric.

10) Cut 7—2½" strips width of fabric for binding.

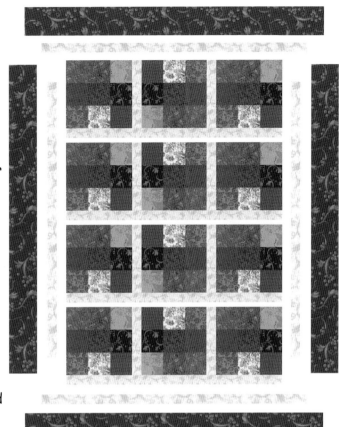

Figure D

Baby Size / Table Topper
40" x 40"

Fabric Requirements:
- 36 charm (5") squares
- ½ yard for 2" sashing
- ½ yard for 3½" border
- 1 1/3 yards for backing
- ½ yard for binding

Cutting Instructions:
1) From sashing fabric, cut 6-2½" strips width of fabric.
   a) Cut 1 of the strips into 2-2½" x 14".
   b) Do not cut the rest of the strips.
2) Cut the border fabric into 4-4" strips width of fabric.

Sewing Instructions:
Same sewing instructions as larger size.

Simply Twisted
56½" x 64½"
30 blocks 8 ½" block
(8" finished)

Now for something a little more adventurous. But don't be fooled, this quilt isn't as hard as it looks. As I stated in the introduction, this is the pattern I designed that got me hooked on charm packs. The emphasis in this quilt is in the placement of light and dark fabrics. Because of this emphasis, there are many other possible settings for the blocks. I like how this setting looks like a 16 patch and a pinwheel, a complicated block set on point, or even a 3-Dimensional design!

Fabric Requirements:
- 120 charm (5") squares
- ½ yard for 2" border
- 1¼ yards for 6" border
- 3 yards for backing
- ½ yard for binding

Cutting Instructions:
1) From 2" border fabric, cut 6-2½" strips width of fabric.
2) From 6" border fabric, cut 6-6½" strips width of fabric.

Sewing Instructions:
1) Divide the 120 charm squares into two groups so there are 60 light fabrics and 60 dark fabrics. Take each of those groups and divide them in half. Now there are 2 sets of 30 light squares and 2 sets of 30 dark squares.

2) Take 60 charm squares (30 lights and 30 darks) and make 60 half square triangles. Use one light square and one dark square for each triangle as shown in Figure A. See Appendix A for instructions on making half square triangles. Square these triangles up to 4½."

Figure A

3) Take the remaining 60 charm squares (30 lights and 30 darks) and make 60 four patch blocks. Make sure the light and dark fabrics alternate as shown in Figure B. There are two ways to make a four patch block from a charm square:

Figure B

   a) One way is to cut each charm square into four 2½" squares. Then switch the lights and darks around and sew them back together into four patch blocks. These four patch blocks should measure 4½".

   b) Another way is to sew them similar to the half square triangle—by drawing a line (not diagonal this time) down the middle vertically and placing it right sides together with another square. Then sew ¼" on either side of the line as shown in Figure C. Next cut on the line and press toward the dark fabric. Match this block up with another block sewn the same way. Make sure the darks are on opposite sides and the seams are butted up against each other. Draw a line perpendicular to the seam and sew on either side of that line. Cutting on this line and pressing yields 2 four patch blocks that should measure $4\frac{1}{2}$".

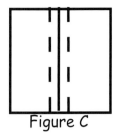

Figure C

4) Now take two of the half square triangles and two of the four patch units and sew together to make one block. Use Figure D to ensure correct placement of the dark and light fabrics. Notice that the triangles are always facing the same direction, but the four patch units are NOT the same.

5) Layout the entire quilt — five blocks across and six blocks down. The quilt requires the same attention to placement as the block does. The blocks are arranged in a pinwheel setting as shown in Figure E. Be sure the lights and darks are always alternating.

Figure D

6) Sew blocks into their 6 strips and sew strips together as shown in Figure E. Your quilt should now measure $40\frac{1}{2}$" x $48\frac{1}{2}$".

7) Take two of the $2\frac{1}{2}$" border strips and cut them in half. Sew each half onto a whole strip. Sew one of these strips onto the left and right sides of the quilt. Then use the other two of these strips to sew on the top and bottom borders. Refer to Appendix B for instructions on applying borders.

8) Sew the outer border on in the same manner using a whole and a half strip for all borders.

9) Refer to Appendix C method 2 to cut and sew the backing fabric.

10) Cut 6—2 $\frac{1}{2}$" strips width of fabric for binding.

Figure E: Lines are placed on the quilt to more easily see block separation.

Simply Untwisted
54½" x 74½"
24 blocks
8 ½" block (8" finished)

Surprisingly, this quilt is almost the same as Simply Twisted. The block is made up of the same elements. This block is created by keeping the four patch unit in the same direction and rotating the half square triangles. Making those simple changes creates an entirely different quilt!

Fabric Requirements:
    96 charm (5") squares
    2/3 yard for sashing
    1/8 yard for cornerstones
    ½ yard for 2" border
    1 1/3 yards for 6" border
    3½ yards for backing
    ½ yard for binding

Cutting Instructions:
1) From cornerstones fabric cut one 2½" strip width of fabric. Cut the strip into 15—2½" squares.
2) From sashing fabric cut 8—2½" strips width of fabric. Cut these strips into 38—2½" x 8½" rectangles.
3) From 2" border fabric, cut 6-2½" strips width of fabric.
4) From 6" border fabric, cut 7-6½" strips width of fabric. Cut one of the strips in half.

Sewing Instructions:
1) Divide the 96 charm squares into two groups so there are 48 light fabrics and 48 dark fabrics. Take each of those groups and divide them in half. Now there are 2 sets of 24 light squares and 2 sets of 24 dark squares.

2) Take 48 charm squares (24 lights and 24 darks) and make 48 half square triangles. Use one light square and one dark square for each triangle as shown in Figure A. See Appendix A for instructions on making half square triangles. Square these triangles up to 4½."

Figure A

3) Take the remaining 48 charm squares (24 lights and 24 darks) and make 48 four patch blocks. Make sure the light and dark fabrics alternate as shown in Figure B. There are two ways to make a four patch block from a charm square:

    a) One way is to cut each charm square into four 2½" squares. Then switch the lights and darks around and sew them back together into

Figure B

four patch blocks. These four patch blocks should measure 4½".
b) Another way is to sew them similar to the half square triangle—by drawing a line (not diagonal this time) down the middle vertically and placing it right sides together with another square. Then sew ¼" on either side of the line as shown in Figure C. Next cut on the line and press toward the dark fabric. Match this block up with another block sewn the same way. Make sure the darks are on opposite sides and the seams are butted up against each other. Draw a line perpendicular to the seam and sew on either side of that line. Cutting on this line and pressing yields 2 four patch blocks that should measure 4½".

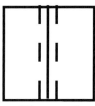

Figure C

4) Now take two of the half square triangles and two of the four patch units and sew together to make one block. Use Figure D to ensure correct placement of the dark and light fabrics.

Figure D

5) Layout the entire quilt — four blocks across and six blocks down. The blocks are arranged as shown in Figure E.

6) Sew 18 of the vertical sashing strips onto the right of the first three blocks in each row. Do not sew a sashing strip onto the last block. Sew blocks into their 6 strips.

7) Sew the rest of the sashing strips and cornerstones into strips as also shown in Figure E. Press seams toward the sashing strips.

6) Sew strips together as shown in Figure E. Your quilt should now measure 38½" x 58½".

7) Take two of the 2½" border strips and sew them together to make one long border strip. Repeat with another pair of strips. Sew one of these double strips onto the left side and another onto the right side of the quilt. Using the 2 remaining border strips, sew on the top and bottom borders. Refer to Appendix B for instructions on applying borders.

8) Sew the outer border on in the same manner using a double strip for the side borders and a whole and a half strip for the top and bottom borders .

9) Refer to Appendix C method 2 to cut and sew the backing fabric

9) Cut 7—2 ½" strips width of fabric for binding.

Figure E

Charming Flowers
52½" x 70½"
24 blocks
9½" block (9" finished)

After a colder than usual winter, I was ready for spring. I was given 4 fat quarters that made me feel hopeful that spring would come. After finding coordinating fabrics in my stash and at the quilt shop, this quilt came about. This was one quilt that I cut my own charm squares out of fat quarters so the flowers looked the same. It would also look fun with each flower being made out of different fabrics of the same color.

Fabric Requirements:
- 96 charm (5") squares
- 1¼ yards for background
- 1/3 yard for flower centers
- ½ yard for 2" border
- 1¼ yards for 6" border
- 3¼ yards for backing
- 2/3 yard for binding

Cutting Instructions:
1) Refer to Commonly Asked Questions number 5 on page 4 for information on cutting charm squares out of fat quarters if you choose.
2) From background fabric, cut 14—2¾" strips width of fabric. Cut strips into 192—2¾" squares.
3) From flower center fabric, cut 5—2" strips width of fabric. Cut strips into 96—2" squares.
4) Cut the inner border fabric into 5—2½" strips width of fabric.
5) Cut the outer border fabric into 6—6½" strips width of fabric.

Sewing Instructions:
1) This quilt is made up of 96 identical petal units. It takes three steps to turn a charm square into a flower petal.

2) First, draw a diagonal line with a pencil on the back of all of the small background squares and the flower centers.

3) Take one of the small background squares. Place it on one corner of a charm square with right sides of the fabric together as shown

Figure A

in Figure A. Sew on the line. Trim seam allowance to $\frac{1}{4}$".

4) Press open as shown in Figure B. Sew all 96 charm squares in this manner.

Figure B

Figure C

5) Take another small background square. Place it on an adjacent corner of a charm square with right sides together. Repeat the same process as in step 3 resulting in the flower petal shown in Figure C.

Figure D

6) Make the flower center using the same process. Flower centers must be sewn onto the same corner of each charm square. As shown in Figure D, the flower center is sewn onto the bottom left corner.

7) Once the petal units are complete, the flowers can be sewn together by rotating the petals around the center as shown in Figure E.

8) Layout the quilt 4 flowers across and 6 flowers down. Sew flowers into rows then sew rows together. The quilt should now measure $36\frac{1}{2}$" x $54\frac{1}{2}$".

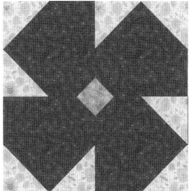
Figure E

9) Cut one of the inner border strips in half. Sew each half onto a whole strip. Sew one of these long strips onto the left side and another onto the right side. Refer to Appendix B for instructions on applying borders. Sew a border strip onto the top and bottom in the same manner.

10) Cut two of the outer border strips in half and sew each half onto a whole strip. Apply outer borders in the same manner as inner borders.

11) Refer to Appendix C method 2 to cut and sew the backing.

12) Cut 7—2 $\frac{1}{2}$" strips width of fabric for binding.

Charming Birds
64½" x 88½"
24 blocks
12 ½" block (12" finished)

Charm squares are the perfect size to make this quilt. I was surprised at the ease with which this quilt went together. By using half square triangles and squaring up along the way, these birds practically "flew" into place. The only thing to watch was sewing the main diagonal seam. With a little precaution, even the bias seam doesn't slow this quilt down.

Fabric Requirements:
  72 charm (5") squares
  2¼ yard for background
  ¾ yard for 2" border
  1½ yards for 6" border
  5 yards for backing
  2/3 yard for binding

Cutting Instructions:
1) Cut background fabric into 5—5" strips width of fabric.
   a) Cut into 36—5" squares.
2) Also cut background fabric into 4—12 7/8" strips width of fabric.
   a) Cut these strips into 12—12 7/8" squares
   b) Cut each square diagonally resulting in 24 triangles.
3) Take 36 of the 5" charm squares and cut them diagonally in half.
4) From 2" border fabric, cut 7-2½" strips width of fabric.
5) From 6" border fabric, cut 8-6½" strips width of fabric.

Sewing Instructions:
1) Take 36 charm squares and 36-5" background squares and make half square triangles. Square up to 4½". Refer to Appendix A for instructions on making half square triangles.

2) Now to sew the birds. Layout 3 half square triangle units and three half charm squares as shown in Figure A. Sew each row together being careful to match the points indicated with a circle. Press seams in the direction of the arrows.

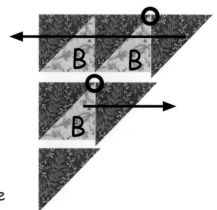

Figure A: B refers to the background fabric.

3) Sew rows together as shown in Figure B. Be careful to match the points indicated with a circle. Press seams in the directions of the arrow. Take care when pressing not to distort the block.

4) Next trim the ¼" seam allowance as shown in Figure B. The dotted line represents the sewing line which goes right through the two corner seams. The solid line represents the cutting line which is ¼" away from the intersections. Line up the ¼" mark on ruler with the two intersections along the long diagonal side of the block and trim.

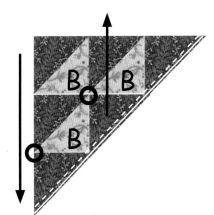

Figure B: B refers to the background fabric.

5) Repeat using all half square triangle units and charm triangles. One block takes 3 half square triangle units and 4 charm triangles. When finished, there will be 24 bird units.

6) To finish off the block, sew the bird unit to a background square as shown in Figure C. This last seam is a long bias seam that likes to stretch. To prevent stretching, place 3-5 pins along the seam. Also, after placing right sides together, stitch with the bird unit on top. This allows care to be taken with the two intersections while sewing.

Figure C

7) Layout quilt as shown in Figure D. This is a rotated setting. There are many other settings to experiment with at this point.

8) After deciding on a layout, sew the blocks in rows of 4. Then sew the rows together as shown in Figure D. Your quilt should now measure 48½" x 72½".

9) Take two of the 2½" border strips and sew them together. Repeat with two more 2½" border strips. Sew one of these strips onto the left and right sides of the quilt.

10) Take one of the 2½" border strips and cut it in half. Sew each half onto a whole strip. Use these two steps to sew on the top and bottom borders. Refer to Appendix B for instructions on applying borders.

11) Sew the outer border on in the same manner using a double strip for all borders.

Figure D

12) Refer to Appendix C method 3 to cut and sew the backing fabric.

13) Cut 8—2 ½" strips width of fabric for binding.

Charming Fat Quarter
37" x 37"

Take a fat quarter, a charm pack, and a little yardage, and this is the result. A friend of mine gave me the idea for this quilt. After she explained it to me, I went home and made two of them! It is a super fast baby quilt or table topper and a fun quilt to buy fabric for.

Fabric Requirements:
- 24 charm (5") squares
- 1 fat quarter (center)
- 2/3 yard borders (6-3" strips)
- 1/3 yard binding
- 1¼ yards backing

Cutting Instructions:
1) Cut fat quarter into 18" square
2) Cut border fabric into 6-3" strips width of fabric.
   a) Cut two strips each into 1-3"x18" and 1-3"x23" so there are two of each size.
   b) Cut two strips into 2-3"x32" strips.
   c) Cut two strips into 2-3"x37" strips.

Sewing Instructions:
1) Sew the 18" border strips to the sides of the center square. Sew the 23" border strips to the top and bottom of the center square.

2) Layout the quilt as shown in Figure A.

3) Next sew the 5 left squares into a strip and the 5 right squares into another strip. Also sew the 7 top squares into one strip and the 7 bottom squares into another strip.

4) Sew the left strip of squares onto the center and the right strip of squares onto the center. Then sew the top and bottom strips of squares onto

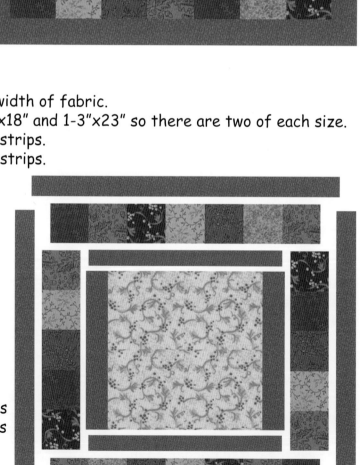

Figure A

the center.
5) Sew the 32" strips onto the left and right sides and the 37" strips onto the top and bottom.
6) Cut 6—2½" strips width of fabric for binding.

Larger Size
49" x 49"

This quilt is perfect to enlarge by adding an extra border.

Fabric Requirements:
24 charm (5") squares
1 fat quarter (center)
2/3 yard for 2½" borders
1 yard for 6½" borders
½ yard binding
2¼ yards backing

Cutting Instructions:
1) Cut fat quarter into 18" square
2) Cut 2½" border fabric into 6-3" strips width of fabric.
   a) Cut two strips each into 1-3"x18" and 1-3"x23" so there are two of each size.
   b) Cut two strips into 2-3"x32" strips.
   c) Cut two strips into 2-3"x37" strips.
3) Cut 6½" border fabric into 5-6½" strips width of fabric.
   a) Cut one of the strips in half.

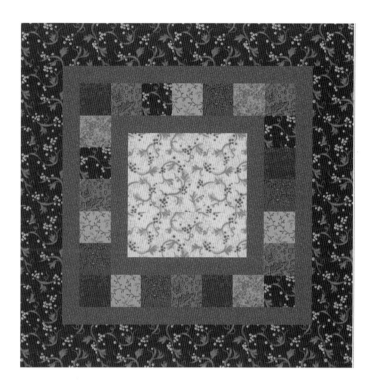

Sewing Instructions:
1) Follow steps 1-5 of the regular size pattern.

2) Take two of the 6½" border strips sew them onto the left side and right side of the quilt.

3) Take the two half 6½" border strips and sew them each onto a whole strip. Sew these two long strips onto the top and bottom of the quilt.

4) Refer to Appendix C method 1 to cut and sew the backing fabric.

5) Cut 5-2½" strips width of fabric for binding.

Charming Queen
86" x 90½"

As I showed some quilters *Charming Fat Quarter*, I was asked how to make the quilt bigger. *Charming Queen* is the result. The center is perfect for a large scale fabric or a panel print.

Fabric Requirements:
 100 charm (5") squares
 1 yard for center
 3½ yard for borders
 6¼ yards for backing
 2/3 yard for binding

Cutting Instructions:
1) Cut center fabric into a rectangle 36" x 40½".
2) Cut border fabric into the following:
 a) 4—3" strips width of fabric,
 b) 6—5" strips width of fabric, and
 c) 8—9½" strips width of fabric.

Sewing Instructions:
1) Take the 4-3" border strips. Sew one to the left side and another to the right side of the center square. Press. Next sew the 3" border strips to the top and bottom of the center square. Press. Refer to Appendix B for instructions on sewing borders.

2) Layout the quilt as shown on the opposite page.

3) Sew the charm squares into strips of 10, 11, 14, or 15 squares as shown in the assembly diagram layout on the opposite page.

4) Next sew the strips of squares to the quilt. Begin by sewing the border strips of 10 squares to the left side and right side. Then sew the border strips of 11 squares to the top and bottom.

5) Continue sewing the borders on as shown in the assembly diagram on the opposite page.

6) Refer to Appendix C method 3 for cutting and sewing the backing.

7) Cut 8—2½" strips for binding.

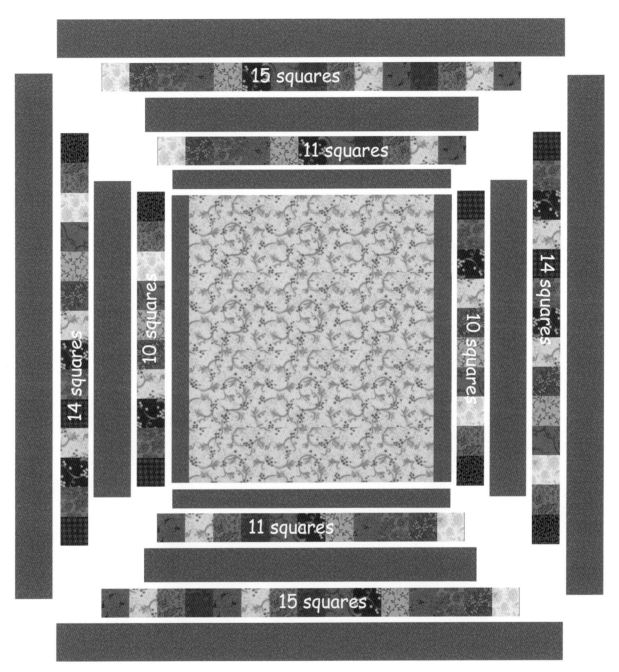

Assembly Diagram

Charming Squares
Finished Size: 76" x 80"

This quilt came about when my friend went to a quilt shop that had a sale on charm packs. (Because of the popularity of charm packs, that really doesn't happen very often.) She, of course, purchased several and wanted to do something simple, but different with them. This quilt is very simple, but the offset sashing creates a unique look.

Fabric Requirements:
- 156 -- 5" charm squares
- 1½ yard sashing and inner border
- 1½ yard outer border
- 5¾ yards backing
- ¾ yard binding

Cutting Instructions:
1) From sashing fabric, cut 15 -- 3" strips width of fabric
   a) Cut 2 of these strips into 2--3" x 32." These are the vertical sashing pieces for the second row.
   b) Cut 2 of these strips into 4--3" x 14." These are the vertical sashing pieces for the first and third rows.
   c) Cut 1 of these strips in half
   d) Set aside the remaining 10 strips
2) From outer border fabric, cut 8--6" strips width of fabric

Sewing Instructions:
1) Layout quilt 12 charm squares across and 13 charm squares down as shown above.

2) Sew the nine square and rectangular pieces together, listed as Blocks A, B, C, and D as shown in Figure A and as listed below:
   - Block A -- 3 squares across and 3 squares down
   - Block B -- 6 squares across and 3 squares down
   - Block C -- 3 squares across and 7 squares down
   - Block D -- 6 squares across and 7 squares down

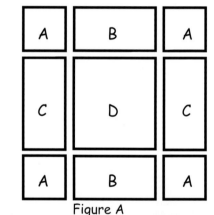

Figure A

3) Sew the vertical sashing pieces onto the right side of the first two blocks in each row as shown in Figure B.

4) Sew each row together. Press towards the sashing strips.

5) Refer to Appendix B for instructions on sewing the sashing and border strips.

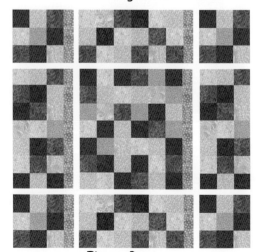

Figure B

Charming Old Maid
Pieced by Midge Hazelgren
Quilted by Konda Luckau

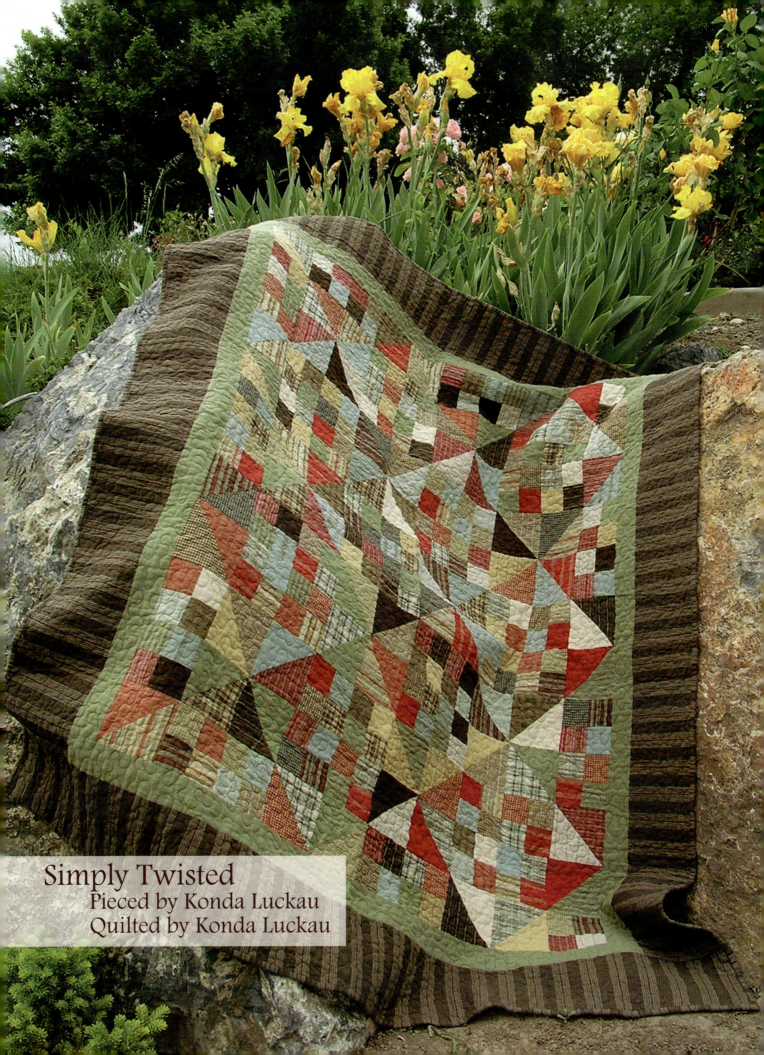

Simply Twisted
Pieced by Konda Luckau
Quilted by Konda Luckau

The Charming Path
Pieced by Andrea McConnell
Quilted by Konda Luckau

Charming Lady
Pieced by Alene Zeeman
Quilted by Konda Luckau

Charming Fat Triangles
Pieced by Marjorie Brown
Quilted by Konda Luckau

Charming Fence
Pieced by Carolyn Rigtrup
Quilted by Konda Luckau

Charming Queen
Pieced by Konda Luckau
Quilted by Konda Luckau

Charming Fat Quarter
Pieced by Konda Luckau
Quilted by Konda Luckau

Charming Baskets
Pieced by Konda Luckau
Quilted by Konda Luckau

Charming Squares
Pieced by Midge Hazelgren
Quilted by Konda Luckau

6) Take the two half sashing strips and sew each of the halves onto a whole strip. These are the horizontal sashing strips.

7) Sew a horizontal sashing strip onto the bottom of the first two rows. Press, again toward the sashing.

8) Sew the rows together as shown in Figure C. The quilt should now measure $59\frac{1}{2}$" x 64."

9) Now there are 8 sashing strips remaining for the inner border. Take two of these strips and sew them together to make one double border strip. Repeat with the remaining border strips. Now there are 4 double border strips.

10) Sew on the inner border using these double border strips. First sew a double strip onto the left side of the quilt and another onto the right side of the quilt. Next sew on of these double strips onto the top of the quilt and the last double strip onto the bottom of the quilt.

11) Sew on the outer border in the same manner.

12) Refer to Appendix C method 3 to cut and sew the backing fabric. (Note: If your backing fabric is a true 44"-45" wide, then method 2 may be used. In which case only $4\frac{1}{2}$ yards of backing fabric is needed.)

13) Cut 8 -- $2\frac{1}{2}$" strips width of fabric for the binding.

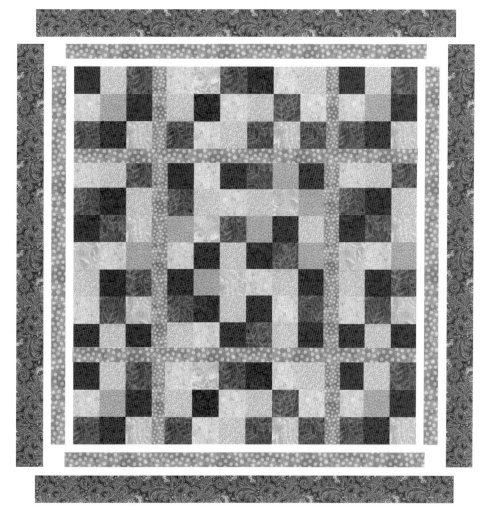

Figure C

Charming Fat Triangles
51" x 51"

This quilt is a variation of the *Charming Fat Quarter* from the book *Simply Charming*. The measurements for the two inner borders are different to compensate for smaller size of the half square triangles. The diagonal lines of the triangles create movement and contrast in this version.

Fabric Requirements:
   28 charm squares
   1 fat quarter
   ¾ yard for inner two borders
   1 yard for outer border
   2½ yards for backing
   ½ yard for binding

Materials Needed:
   4½" ruler

Cutting Instructions:
1) Cut fat quarter into an 18" x 18" square.
2) Cut inner border fabric into 6 -- 3¾" strips width of fabric.
   a) Cut two strips each into:
      1 -- 3¾" x 18" and 1 -- 3¾" x 24½"
   b) Cut two strips into 2 -- 3¾" x 32½"
   c) Cut two strips into 2 -- 3¾" x 39"
3) Cut outer border fabric into 5 -- 6½" strips width of fabric.
   a) Cut one in half.

Sewing Instructions:
1) Take all 28 charm squares and separate them into 14 light squares and 14 dark squares.

2) Use all 28 charm squares to make 28 half square triangles. Refer to Appendix A for instructions on making half square triangles. Use one light square and one dark square for each half square triangle as shown in Figure A.

Figure A

3) Square up to 4½."

4) Sew the two 3¾" x 18" rectangles onto the left side and right side of the fat quarter as shown in Figure B.

5) Sew the two 3¾" x 24½" rectangles onto top and bottom of the fat quarter as also shown in Figure B.

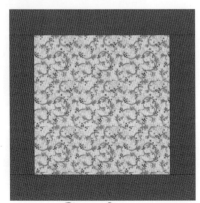

Figure B

6) Lay out the quilt as shown in Figure C. Note that all of the half square triangles are oriented in the same direction.

7) Sew the 6 half square triangles from the left side of the quilt into a strip. Sew the 6 half square triangles from the right side of the quilt into a strip.

8) Sew the 8 half square triangles from the top of the quilt into a strip. Sew the 8 half square triangles from the bottom of the quilt into a strip.

9) Sew the left and right strips of half square triangles onto the quilt.

10) Next sew the top and bottom strips of half square triangles onto the quilt.

11) Take the 2 -- 3¾" x 32½" border pieces and sew them onto the left side and right side of the quilt.

12) Take the 2 -- 3¾" x 39" border pieces and sew them onto the top and bottom of the quilt.

13) Refer to Appendix B for instructions on sewing borders. Take 2 of the 6½" border strips and sew one onto the left side of the quilt and the other onto the right side of the quilt.

14) Take the two half 6½" border strips and sew each one of them onto a whole strip. Sew one of these long strips onto the top of the quilt. Sew the other long strip onto the bottom of the quilt.

15) Refer to Appendix C method 1 to cut and sew the backing fabric.

16) Cut 6 -- 2½" strips width of fabric for binding.

Figure C

Charming Fence
64" x 64"
36 blocks
8½" block (8" finished)

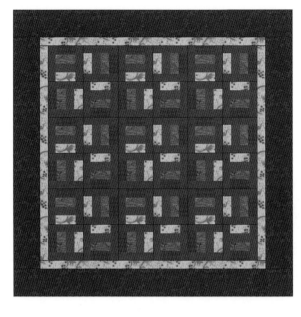

I was trying to figure out a way to make the classic rail fence pattern using charm packs when this quilt came about. The odd measurements of the side strips create a square block that can be rotated. This pattern is fun with a low contrast background, as the one shown, as well as with a high contrast background.

Fabric Requirements:
- 72 charm squares
- 1¼ yard for background fabric
- ½ yard inner border
- 1½ yard outer border
- 4 yards backing
- ¾ yard binding

Cutting Instructions:
1) Cut 15 -- 2¼" strips from background fabric
   a) Cut all 15 strips into 72 -- 2¼" x 8½" rectangles (there will be 3 extra)
2) Cut 6 -- 2½" strips for inner border. Cut two of these in half.
3) Cut 7 -- 6½" strips for outer border. Cut one of these in half.

Sewing Instructions:
1) Randomly divide the 72 charm squares into two groups of 36. Draw a **vertical** line down the middle of half of the charm squares as shown in Figure A.

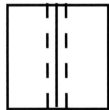

Figure A

2) Pair a charm square with a line drawn on it with a charm square that does not have a line drawn on it. Place right sides together and sew a ¼" seam on both sides of the line as also shown in Figure A.

3) Cut on the line. Press seam allowance to one side. The result is two blocks similar to Figure B. Repeat with all charm squares.

Figure B

4) Randomly sew two of these pairs together into a strip of four as shown in Figure C. Repeat with all pairs.

Figure C

5) Sew a 2¼" x 8½" rectangle onto either side of the strip of charms as shown in Figure D. Press seam allowance toward the background strips.

6) Layout blocks 6 across and 6 down rotating every other block as shown in Figure E.

7) Sew blocks into 6 rows.

8) Sew rows together. The quilt should now measure 48½" x 48½."

9) Take the 2½" inner border strips. Sew each of the 4 halves onto a whole length.

10) Refer to Appendix B for instructions on applying borders. Sew one of these border strips onto the left side of the quilt and another onto the right side of the quilt. Next sew one of the border strips onto the top of the quilt and another onto the bottom of the quilt.

11) Take the 6½" outer border strips. Take the 2 half strips and sew each of them onto a whole length. Take these two strips and sew one onto the left side of the quilt and another onto the right side of the quilt.

Figure D

12) Take the remaining 4 -- 6½" outer border strips. Sew two of them together to make a double strip. Take the remaining two and sew them together as well.

13) Sew one of these double strips onto the top of the quilt and another onto the bottom of the quilt.

14) Refer to Appendix C method 2 to cut and sew backing.

15) Cut 7 -- 2½" strips width of fabric for binding.

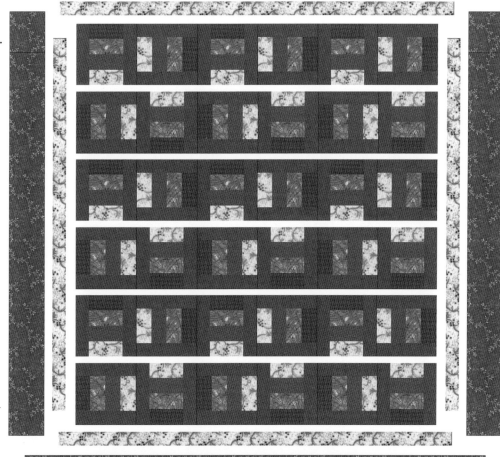

Figure E

The Charming Path
95" x 95"
16 blocks
18½" block (18" finished)

The Charming Path is made from both fat quarters and charm packs. This is a quick quilt to put together because there are no matching seams in adjacent blocks. The scrappy border was the serendipitous result of the leftover pieces from the fat quarters. It adds a fun finishing touch.

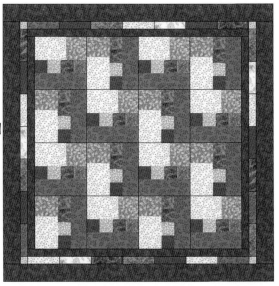

Fabric Requirements:
- 64 charm squares
- 16 fat quarters
- 2½ yards for borders
- 7½ yards for backing
- ¾ yard for binding

Cutting Instructions:
1) Cut 8 -- 3" strips width of fabric for inner border
2) Cut 9 -- 6¾" strips width of fabric for outer border.
   a) Cut one of these strips in half.
3) Cut all fat quarters as shown in the Figure A and as follows:
   a) Cut 1 -- 6" strip width of fabric
      Trim to 6" x 18½"
   b) Cut 1 -- 8½" strip width of fabric
      Cut strip into 1 -- 8½" x 7½" and 1 -- 8½" x 11½"
   c) Cut 1 -- 3" strip and set aside for second border

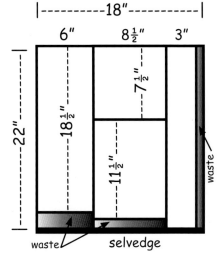

Figure A

Sewing Instructions:
1) Randomly take one of the 8½" x 7½" rectangles and one of the 8½" x 11½" rectangles and sew them together as shown in Figure B. Repeat with all 8½" x 7½" and 8½" x 11½" rectangles.

Figure B

2) Randomly sew together the charm squares into strips of 4 charm squares as shown in Figure C. Use all 64 charm squares to make 16 strips of charm squares. Press the seam allowances in one direction.

3) Assemble blocks as shown in Figure D. Press seam allowances away from the charm squares.

Figure C

Figure D

4) Lay out the quilt rotating the blocks as shown in Figure E.

5) Sew blocks into four rows.

6) Sew rows together as shown in Figure E. The quilt should now measure $72\frac{1}{2}"$ x $72\frac{1}{2}."$

7) Take two of the 3" inner border strips and sew them together to make a double border strip. Repeat with the six remaining 3" border strips making four double border strips.

8) Refer to Appendix B for instructions on applying borders. Sew one of the double strips onto the left side of the quilt and and another onto the right side of the quilt. Next sew a double strip onto the top and bottom of the quilt.

9) Take the 3" strips previously set aside from the fat quarters. Cut each of these into two pieces of random lengths approximately 3" x 5" to 3" x 9."

10) Sew these 3" fat quarter pieces of random lengths into four long border strips. Two of these strips need to be at least $77\frac{1}{2}"$ and two of these strips need to be at least $82\frac{1}{2}."$ Press.

11) Sew the two shorter strips (at least $77\frac{1}{2}"$) onto the left side of the quilt and the right side of the quilt. Then sew the two longer strips (at least $82\frac{1}{2}"$) onto the top and bottom of the quilt.

12) Next take the $6\frac{3}{4}"$ outer border strips. Sew each of the two half border strips onto a whole strip. Sew another whole strip onto these strips. Take two of the remaining border strips and sew them together to create a double strip. Repeat with the last two border strips. Now there will be two double strips and two double and a half strips.

13) Sew one double strips onto the left side and another double strip onto the right side of the quilt. Then sew one of the double and a half strips onto the top of the quilt and the other double and a half strip onto the bottom of the quilt.

14) Refer to Appendix C method 3 to cut and sew the backing fabric.

15) Cut 9 -- $2\frac{1}{2}"$ strips width of fabric for the binding.

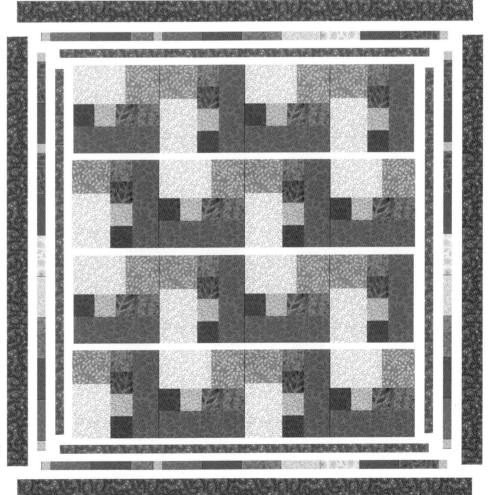

Figure E

Charming Old Maid
68" x 92"
24 blocks
12½" block (12" finished)

This classic block has several names, I thought "Old Maid" was the funnest one. This is a very versatile block. You may want to play around with the layout and rotation of the blocks. Although the layout shown is the one I chose, you may like a different one better. *Charming Old Maid* works well with a background that has a good contrast from the charm pack. This charm pack had many medium and dark fabrics so a light background worked well. If your charm pack contains a lot of light and medium fabrics, you may like a dark background.

Fabric Requirements:
- 72 charm squares
- 2½ yards background fabric
- 1 yard inner border
- 2 yards outer border
- 5¾ yards backing
- ¾ yard binding

Materials Needed:
- 4½" ruler

Cutting Instructions:
1) Cut 9-5" strips from background fabric width of fabric.
   a) Cut these strips into 72-5" squares.
2) Cut 9-4½" strips from background fabric width of fabric.
   a) Cut these strips into 72-4½" squares.
3) Cut 7--3½" strips for inner border width of fabric.
   a) Cut one of these in half.
4) Cut 8--7½" strips for outer border width of fabric.

Sewing Instructions:
1) Take all 72 charm squares and all 72--5" background squares.

Use all of these squares to make 144 half square triangles. Refer to Appendix A for instructions on making half square triangles. Use one charm square and one background square for each half square triangle as shown in Figure A.

2) Square up to 4½."

3) Layout block as shown in Figure B noting the orientation of the half square triangles. Each block uses 6 of the half square triangles and three of the 4½" background squares.

4) Sew the squares into rows. Press seam allowances in the direction of the arrows shown in Figure B.

5) Sew rows together into a block.

Figure A

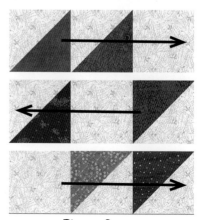

Figure B

6) Repeat with all half square triangles and 4½" background squares to make a total of 24 blocks.

7) Layout blocks, 4 blocks across and 6 blocks down, as shown in Figure C. Note the rotation of the blocks.

8) Sew blocks into 6 rows.

9) Sew rows together. The quilt should now measure 48½" x 72½"

10) Refer to Appendix B for instructions on applying borders. Take the 3½" inner border strips. Sew each of the 2 half strips onto a whole length. Sew the remaining four strips into two double strips.

11) Take one of the long double strips and sew it onto the left side of the quilt. Sew another double strip onto the right side of the quilt. Next sew one of the shorter strips onto the top of the quilt and another shorter strip onto the bottom of the quilt.

12) Take the 7½" outer border strips. Take two of the whole strips and sew them together. Repeat with the 6 remaining strips making four double strips.

13) Take one of these double strips and sew it onto the left side of the quilt. Then sew another double strip onto the right side of the quilt.

14) Sew a third double strip onto the top of the quilt and the last double strip onto the bottom of the quilt.

15) Refer to Appendix A method 3 to cut and sew the backing fabric.

16) Cut 8--2½" strips width of fabric for the binding.

Figure C: Lines are placed on the quilt to more easily see block separation.

Charming Lady
92" x 92"
24 blocks
16½" block (16" finished)

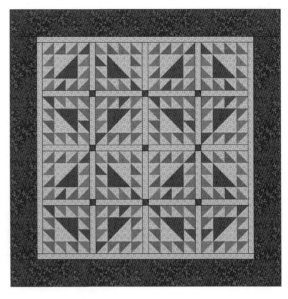

From the *Charming Old Maid* to the *Charming Lady*, I love the names of quilt blocks. This classic block is called "Lady of the Lake." Like the *Charming Old Maid*, this quilt also benefits from a background with high contrast with the charm square fabrics. Four of these blocks would make a nice wall hanging. Another variation that would be fun is to take out the sashing. That would create a secondary design with flying geese units through the quilt.

Fabric Requirements:
    96 charm squares
    ¾ yard fabric for the large dark triangles
    3¾ yards background fabric (includes sashing and inner border)
    2¾ yards outer border fabric (includes cornerstones)
    7 yards backing
    ¾ yard binding

Materials Needed:
    4½" ruler

Cutting Instructions:
1) Cut 12--5" strips width of fabric from the background fabric.
    a) Cut these strips into 96--5" squares.
2) Cut 2--9" strips width of fabric from the background fabric.
    a) Cut these strips into 8--9" squares.
3) Cut 20--2½" strips width of fabric from the background fabric.
    a) Cut 12 of these strips into 24- 2½" x 16½" rectangles (for sashing).
    b) Set aside 8 strips for the inner border.
4) Cut 2--9" strips width of fabric from the dark center triangle fabric.
    a) Cut these strips into 8--9" squares.
5) Cut 1--2½" strip width of fabric from the outer border fabric.
    a) Cut into 9--2½" squares for the cornerstones.
6) Cut 9--9½" strips width of fabric for the outer border.
    a) Cut one of these strips in half.

Sewing Instructions:
1) Take all 96 charm squares and all 96--5" background squares. Use all of these squares to make 192 half square triangles. Refer to Appendix A for instructions on making half square triangles. Use one charm square and one background square for each half square triangle as shown in Figure A.
2) Square up to 4½."
3) With all 8--9" dark triangle squares and all 8--9" background squares, make 16 half square triangles using the same method. Square up to 8½."

Figure A

4) Layout blocks as shown in Figure B. Note that **all** of the half squares triangles are all going in the same direction.

5) Assemble the block as shown in Figure B. Press in the direction of the arrows.

6) Layout quilt as shown in Figure C. Note the block rotation.

7) Sew a 2½" x 16½" sashing piece to the right side of the first three blocks in each row. Do not sew a sashing piece onto the last block of each row.

8) Sew blocks into 4 rows as shown in Figure C. Press seam allowances towards the sashing.

9) Take 9 of the sashing pieces. Sew a cornerstone onto the right side of each sashing piece.

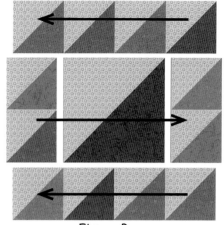

Figure B

10) Take three of these sashing/cornerstone sets and one sashing strip without a cornerstone and sew into a row as shown in Figure C.

11) Sew rows together. The quilt should now measure 70½" x 70½."

12) Take the 8 inner border strips. Take two of these strips and sew them together to make one double strip. Repeat with all inner border strips to make 4 double strips.

13) Refer to Appendix B for instructions on applying borders. Take one of these double strips and sew it onto the left side of the quilt. Sew another double strip onto the right side of the quilt.

14) Next take the 9½" outer border strips. Sew each of the two half pieces onto a whole strip. Sew another whole strip onto these strips. Take two of the remaining border strips and sew them together to create a double strip. Repeat with the last two border strips. Now there will be two double strips and two double and a half strips.

15) Sew one double strips onto the left side and another double onto the right side of the quilt. Then sew one of the double and a half strips onto the top and the other double and a half strip onto the bottom of the quilt.

16) Refer to Appendix C method 3 to cut and sew the backing fabric.

17) Cut 9--2½" strips width of fabric for the binding.

Figure C

Charming Baskets
68½" x 84½"
12 blocks
16½" block (16" finished)

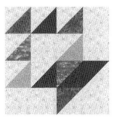

The basket is another classic block, but one I have never been very interested in making. That is until this year. In one of my quilt guilds, a friend of mine was doing a block of the month pattern that was all baskets. Month after month, she would show us fun variations of the basket. While I loved her patterns, I wanted to make my own basket block with charm squares. April Cornell's *Sunshine* fabric line for Moda turned out to be the perfect fabric for making my baskets. I used the prints and the woven fabrics for added variety.

Fabric Requirements:
- 66 charm squares
- 2½ yards background fabric
- 1 yard for 3" inner border
- 2 yards for 7" outer border
- 5¾ yards backing
- ¾ yard binding

Materials Needed:
- 4½" ruler

Cutting Instructions:
1) Cut 4--5" strips width of fabric from the background fabric.
    a) Cut these strips into 30--5" squares.
2) Cut 5--4½" strips width of fabric from the background fabric
    a) Cut these strips into 24--4½" x 8½" rectangles
3) Cut 4--8⅞" strips width of fabric from the background fabric
    a) Cut these strips into 12--8⅞" squares.
    b) Cut these squares in half diagonally
4) Cut 7--3½" strips width of fabric from the inner border fabric
    a) Cut one of these strips in half
5) Cut 8--7½" strips width of fabric from the outer border fabric

Sewing Instructions:
1) Take 30 of the charm squares and all 30 of the 5" background squares.

Use all of these squares to make 60 half square triangles. Refer to Appendix A for instructions on making half square triangles. Use one charm square and one background square for each half square triangle as shown in Figure A. Square up to 4½."

Figure A

2) Take 12 of the charm squares. Use all of these squares to make 12 half square triangles. Use two charm squares for each half square triangle. Square up to 4½."

3) Take the remaining 48 charm squares and cut them in half diagonally.

4) Take 12 of the charm squares that have been cut in half. Sew them to 12 of the 4½" x 8½" rectangles as shown in Figure B.

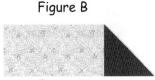

Figure B

Figure C

5) Take 12 of the charm squares that have been cut in half. Sew them to 12 of the 4½" x 8½" rectangles as shown in Figure C. This step is very similar to the previous step, but it is different.

6) Now for the center square section. Take the 12 half square triangles

made from 2 charm squares. Also take the remaining 24 charm squares that have been cut in half. Sew one half charm square to the left of one half square triangle as shown in Figure D being careful to match the points indicated with a circle. Press seam allowance away from the half square triangle.

7) Sew another half charm square to the top of the half square triangle as also shown in Figure D, being careful to match the points indicated with a circle. Press seam allowance away from the half square triangle.

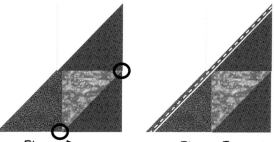

Figure D   Figure E

8) This triangle unit needs to be trimmed. Refer to Figure E. The solid line represents the edge of the ruler. The dotted line represents the cutting line. Line up the $\frac{1}{4}$" mark of the ruler at the point where the three blocks intersect. Also line up the ruler to run parallel to the seam of the half square triangle. Trim carefully.

9) Repeat to make 12 triangle units. Pair up each of these units with an $8\frac{7}{8}$" background triangle. Pin and sew carefully. This seam will stretch easily. Press towards the background triangle. There will be 12 of the center square sections as shown in Figure F.

10) Assemble the block as shown in the assembly diagram in Figure G. Press.

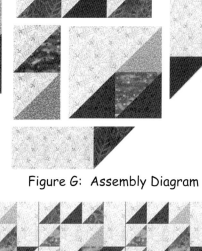

Figure F

Figure G: Assembly Diagram

11) The bottom right corner of the block needs to be trimmed just like the triangle units were trimmed in step 8 as shown in Figure E.

12) Then take the remaining 12--$8\frac{7}{8}$" half squares and sew them onto the bottom right of each block that was just trimmed. Pin and sew carefully. Press toward the background triangle.

13) Layout the quilt as shown in Figure H with 3 blocks across and 4 blocks down.

14) Sew blocks into 4 rows.

15) Sew rows together. The quilt should now measure $48\frac{1}{2}$" x $64\frac{1}{2}$."

16) Refer to Appendix B for instructions on applying borders. Take the $3\frac{1}{2}$" inner border strips. Sew each of the 2 half strips onto a whole length. Sew the remaining four strips into two double strips.

17) Take one of the long double strips and sew it onto the left side of the quilt. Sew another double strip onto the right side of the quilt. Next sew one of the shorter strips onto the top of the quilt and another shorter strip onto the bottom of the quilt.

18) Take the $7\frac{1}{2}$" outer border strips. Take two of the whole strips and sew them together. Repeat with the 6 remaining strips making four double strips.

19) Take one of these double strips and sew it onto the left side. Then sew another double strip onto the right side of the quilt.

20) Sew a third double strip onto the top of the quilt and the last double strip onto the bottom of the quilt.

21) Refer to Appendix A method 3 to cut and sew the backing fabric.

22) Cut 8--$2\frac{1}{2}$" strips width of fabric for the binding.

Figure H

Charming Lonestar
76" x 76"

Fabric often inspires me as I am sure it does many of you. Recently some absolutely gorgeous fabric lines have come out with a large variation of prints and colorways. In these larger charm packs, I found that there were enough fabrics to make a scrappy lonestar quilt. The construction of the Charming Lonestar is super simple too. There are no set in seams; it's made of half square triangles! The secret with making this quilt is labeling all of your fabrics.

The way the pattern is written, you need four squares of each color. Four charm packs will be enough if the charm pack has at least 31 squares in it. I have never dared make a lonestar quilt before, but this one works up so quick that I am not scared anymore. You can decide if you want to tell your friends how simple this pattern really is.

Fabric Requirements:
    124 charm squares (4 charm packs for color placement)
    72 charm squares for lonestar
    52 charm squares for border
    $1\frac{1}{4}$ yards background
    $\frac{3}{4}$ yard for inner border
    $1\frac{3}{4}$ yard for outer border
    $4\frac{1}{2}$ yards for backing
    $\frac{3}{4}$ yard for binding

Materials Needed:
    $4\frac{1}{2}$" ruler

Cutting Instructions:
1) Cut the background fabric into 1--$12\frac{1}{2}$" strip and 2--$12\frac{7}{8}$" strips width of fabric.
    a) Cut the $12\frac{1}{2}$" strip into 3--$12\frac{1}{2}$" squares.
    b) Cut one of the $12\frac{7}{8}$" strips into 3--$12\frac{7}{8}$" squares.
    c) Cut the other $12\frac{7}{8}$" strip into 1--$12\frac{7}{8}$" square and 1--$12\frac{1}{2}$" square.
    d) Cut the 4--$12\frac{7}{8}$" squares diagonally in half.
2) Cut inner border fabric into 6--$3\frac{1}{2}$" strips width of fabric.
    a) Cut two of these strips in half.
3) Cut the outer border fabric into 8--7" strips width of fabric.

Figure A

Sewing Instructions:
1) Take 72 charm squares and separate them into 5 color groups of the following amounts beginning from the tips of the star and working in:
    8 of 1st color, 4 each of 2 similar fabrics
    16 of the 2nd color, 4 each of 4 similar fabrics
    24 of the 3rd color, 4 each of 6 similar fabrics
    16 of the 4th color, 4 each of 4 similar fabrics
    8 of the 5th color, 4 each of 2 similar fabrics
2) Pay careful attention to the layout of this quilt. Refer often to the numbered chart on page 24. There are only three different blocks (A, B, and C) to be made as shown in Figure A. Four of each of the three blocks will be made.

3) Take your 72 charm squares that have been divided into 5 color groups. Decide which fabric will correspond to each number on the chart on page 24. Label each fabric. I like to use painter's tape. Post-it notes or pins and paper work well also.

4) Take 2 (NOT all 4) charm squares of fabric 1a, 1b, 2a, 2d, 3a, and 3f and cut them in half diagonally. Set these aside for later.

5) Refer to the numbered charts to sew half square triangles together as follows:

　a) Looking at the chart, one of the squares is labeled 1b/2c. This means that you need to take 1 square of the fabric labeled 1b and 1 square of fabric labeled 2c and make a half square triangle unit with these two fabrics. Refer to Appendix A for instructions on making half square triangles.

　b) This will make two half square triangle units with these two fabrics. A total of four half square triangle units are needed. Repeat the previous step with one more square of fabric 1b and one more square of fabric 2c. Now there are four half square triangle units with these two fabrics which is the amount needed.

　c) Follow the same method for each of the squares on the chart. Taking two charm squares of each of the two numbers in the square will result in four half square triangles, which is the amount needed.

　d) Square up all of these half square triangles to $4\frac{1}{2}$." There will be 60 half square triangles (four each of 15 different half square triangles). As you make these half square triangles, either keep them labeled or arrange them in their assigned location according to the page 24 chart.

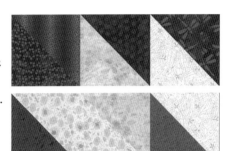

6) First layout Block A according to the chart on page 24. Sew Block A together as shown in Figure B.

Figure B

7) Repeat, making three more identical blocks giving a total of four of Block A.

8) Next layout the bottom section of Block B, with three half square triangles and 3 of the charm squares previously set aside in step 4, according to the chart on page 24 and as shown in Figure C.

9) Sew each row together as shown in Figure C being careful to match the points indicated with circles. Press seams in the direction of the arrows.

10) Next sew the rows together as shown in Figure D once again matching points highlighted with circles and pressing seams in the direction of the arrow.

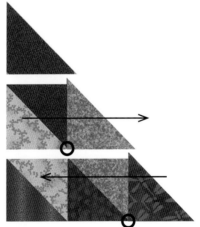

Figure C

11) This triangle unit needs to be trimmed. Refer to Figure D. The solid line represents the edge of the ruler. The dotted line represents the cutting line. Line up the $\frac{1}{4}$" mark of the ruler at the two points where the blocks intersect along the long side of the triangle. Trim carefully.

12) Repeat, making three more identical triangle units giving a total of 4 of Block B triangle units.

13) Sew each of these triangles to the $12\frac{7}{8}$" background triangles as

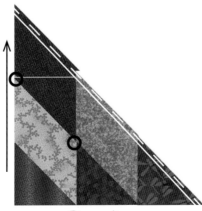

Figure D

Figure E

shown in Figure E. This seam is along a bias edge so pinning is recommended. Be careful not to stretch the seam as sewing. Press toward the background.

14) Sew together four of Block C using the same method described in steps 8-13.

15) Now all the blocks are done. Layout the quilt as shown in Figure F.

16) Sew the blocks into 4 rows. Then sew the four rows together. The quilt should now measure $48\frac{1}{2}$" x $48\frac{1}{2}$."

17) Take the $3\frac{1}{2}$" inner border strips. Sew each of the four half strips onto a whole strip.

18) Sew on the inner border first onto the left side of the quilt and then onto right side of the quilt.

19) Next sew one of these strips onto the top of the quilt and then onto the bottom of the quilt.

20) Take the 52 charm squares that are leftover and sew them into two strips of 12 charm squares and two strips of 14 charm squares.

21) Sew the strips of 12 charm squares onto left side and right side of the quilt. Next sew the strips of 14 charm squares onto the top of the quilt and the bottom of the quilt.

22) Take the 7" outer border strips. Sew two of them together. Repeat with the rest of the outer border strips making four double strips.

23) Sew one of these double strips onto the left side of the quilt and another one onto the right side of the quilt.

24) Take the other two long strips and sew one of them onto the top of the quilt and the last one onto the bottom of the quilt.

25) Refer to Appendix C method 2 to cut and sew the backing fabric together.

26) Cut binding into 8--$2\frac{1}{2}$" strips width of fabric.

Figure F

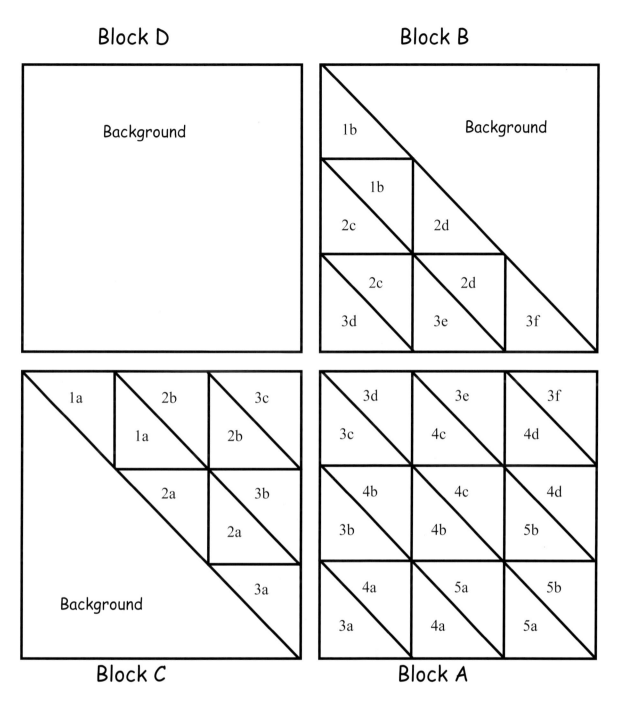

Make 4 of each of these blocks.

Appendix A: Half Square Triangles

This is one method for making half-square triangles. This method uses two squares of the same size and results in two half square triangles. A $\frac{1}{4}$" presser foot is required for this method unless there is a $\frac{1}{4}$" mark on the front of a different presser foot. Guides on the sewing machine do not work with this method. The other tool required is a square ruler the size that the unit is being squared up to. With all the quilts in this book, that would be a $4\frac{1}{2}$" square ruler. A slightly larger square ruler will also work, but is not quite as quick.

Sewing Instructions:
1) Take two different colored squares of the same size. All the quilts in this book start with 5" charm squares.

2) On the back of one square, draw a diagonal line with a pencil that connects two opposite corners of the square as shown by the solid line in Figure A.

3) Pin this square to the second square so right sides of the fabric are together and the pencil line is showing.

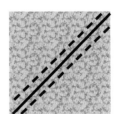

Figure A

4) Sew a $\frac{1}{4}$" seam on either side of the line as shown by the dotted lines in Figure A. With a $\frac{1}{4}$" presser foot, the pencil line will line up on the edge of the presser foot.

5) Cut along the pencil line with a rotary cutter or scissors. Press. Generally seams are pressed towards the dark triangle as shown in Figure B. To press half square triangle units, first press shut with the dark triangle on top. Next lift the dark fabric up and finger press open. Press gently taking care to lift and press with the iron rather than "ironing" the fabric. Ironing will distort the fabric while pressing will not.

Figure B

6) Repeat with the other triangle. Now there are two half square triangle units that need to be squared up.

Squaring Up Instructions:
1) All of the half square triangles in this book will be "squared up" to $4\frac{1}{2}$". Often after sewing half square triangles, these units will be a little skewed. Starting with a 5" charm square gives an $\frac{1}{8}$" to trim the unit into a $4\frac{1}{2}$" square. Generally that $\frac{1}{8}$" is just the right amount of extra fabric for squaring up.

2) Before squaring up, the half square triangle unit must be pressed as explained in step 6 above. Then place one half square triangle unit on a cutting mat right side up. Take a $4\frac{1}{2}$" square ruler and place it on top of the unit. Match the ruler to the unit in two places. First match opposite corners of the ruler to the diagonal seam of the half square triangle. Second look around the edges of the ruler and make sure the unit either lines up with the ruler or sticks out a little from underneath.

3) Hold ruler firmly. With a rotary cutter trim the right and top sides along the ruler. Carefully turn the unit and the ruler to trim the other two sides.

4) Now the half square triangle unit is a perfect $4\frac{1}{2}$" square as shown in Figure C that will sew nicely into any pattern!

Figure C

Appendix B: Midge's Perfect Borders and Sashing

Care must be taken when sewing on long pieces of fabric. This method of applying sashing and borders is perfect for the beginning (and experienced) quilter. Using this method will ensure sashing and border lay flat. They will not be too tight leaving a "pregnant" quilt, and they will not be too loose leaving borders that ripple and wave. What it does not do is ensure that a quilt is square. This method maintains the shape of the interior of the quilt. So if your blocks and rows are square and pressed neatly, this method will preserve those square angles and your entire quilt will remain square. The sewing instructions will be given for applying borders. This method also works for sewing on long sashing strips.

Preparation:
1) Press everything neatly. Press blocks that sashing will be applied to and press the entire quilt that borders will be applied to.

2) Make sure the sashing or border strips are a little longer than the blocks or quilt they are being applied to and that they are also free of creases.

3) The only tools you need are pins. Have plenty on hand.

Sewing Instructions:
1) Stand up. First we will pin the left border. Line up the top left corner of the quilt and the end of the first border strip right sides together. Pin.

2) Hold the pinned area and gently shake the quilt and the border. This allows gravity to help line up the quilt and border for a few more inches. Pin. Take care not to stretch either the quilt or the border. Continue down the border by holding the next pin, shaking out, lining up the quilt and border, and placing the next pin. Pin approximately every 8".

3) After the border is pinned, trim the border even with the end of the quilt. Take care to make this cut straight and square to prevent "dog-eared" corners.

4) Sew on border with a $\frac{1}{4}$" seam allowance. Take care not to stretch either the quilt or the border. Holding onto the pins while sewing will prevent uneven stretching. Press.

5) Repeat with the right border and then with the top and bottom borders. Generally borders are applied in this order:
       1) left and right inside borders
       2) top and bottom inside borders
       3) left and right outside borders
       4) top and bottom outside borders

If there are more borders, they are added in the same order with left and right borders generally added before top and bottom borders.

6) Viola! A few pins and standing up to let gravity help makes quick work out of long unruly borders and sashing strips.

Appendix C: Piecing a Back

Many quilt shops carry backing fabric that is 90" wide or 108" wide which is handy because it eliminates the need to piece a back for the quilt. This fabric is usually very reasonably priced. However, for many reasons, quilters often need to seam fabric together to make a back large enough for the back of a quilt.

First, when figuring out how to seam a back, be sure the back is several inches larger both in the length and the width than the quilt top. If the quilt is 40" (sometimes 42") wide or smaller, then one length of fabric will be enough. The following examples apply when the width is greater than 40". Then we need to take the length into consideration when deciding how to piece the back together.

1) **Length of the quilt is between 40" and 60"**
   ~Take the width of the fabric and round up to a nice number. That is the whole length. To find the rest of the fabric needed, take half of that amount and add it to the whole length. That is how much fabric needs to be purchased.
   ~Cut the fabric into 2 pieces--one piece will be the "whole" length and the second piece will be the "half" length. Take the "half" length and cut it in half lengthwise. Lengthwise is the long side that is parallel to the selvedge. This cut will often be made on or close to the fold put in the fabric by the manufacturer.
   ~Sew the two short sides of this "half" length together so that now it is as long as the "whole" length. Sew onto the two lengths together as shown in Figure A.

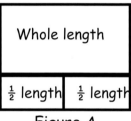
Figure A

2) **Length of the quilt is between 60" and 80"**
   ~Most of the quilts in this book require this type of seaming. It is also the quickest.
   ~Take the width of the fabric and round up to a nice number. That is the whole length.
   ~Two lengths are need so the amount is doubled. That is how much fabric needs to be purchased.
   ~Cut the fabric in half so there are two "whole" lengths.
   ~Sew the two lengths together along the selvedge as shown in Figure B.

Figure B

3) **Length of the quilt is between 80" and 100"**
   ~Take the width of the fabric and round up to a nice number. That is the whole length. To find the rest of the fabric needed, take half of that amount and add it to TWO whole lengths. That is how much fabric needs to be purchased.
   ~Cut the fabric into two "whole" lengths and one "half" length.
   ~Take the "half" length and cut it in half lengthwise. Lengthwise is the long side that is parallel to the selvedge. This cut will often be made on or close to the fold put in the fabric by the manufacturer.
   ~Sew the two short sides of this "half" length together so that now it is as long as the "whole" length. Sew onto the three lengths together as shown in Figure C.

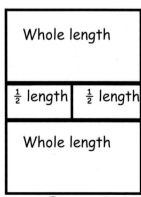
Figure C